10歳のあなた
と
10歳だったあなたへ

〜聖霊からのおくりもの〜

Prema 🌻 陽子

あなたはこの世界(せかい)に生まれた。

宇宙(うちゅう)の中の地球(ちきゅう)という星(ほし)の

この体(いのち)に生命(いのち)を宿(やど)した。

生命(いのちたましい)(魂)は永遠(えいえん)のもの

そして、

すべては一(ひと)つ。

You were born to this world.

In the universe on a planet

called earth

your soul has been carried in

your body.

Your soul is eternal

and

All is One.

あなたは10歳になりました。

あなたはこれから人生の旅に出ます。

人生で宝物を探す旅に出るのです。

その門出をとても嬉しく思います。

You are now ten years old.

You are about to start your journey of life…

a journey to find your treasures in life.

I am delighted to celebrate your departure.

Preface

*This book is a message from the Holy Spirit.
This book came into your possession, because the Holy Spirit wishes you to read this message.
It is a blessing from the Holy Spirit that you encountered this book. It is a miracle.*

What is written in this book

💗 *The Kingdom of Children*

💗 *Beginning of a Journey ~Dandelion Puff~*

💗 *About Treasures*

💗 *To Be Happy*

💗 *Whereabouts of Peace* 🍀

はじめに

この本の内容は、聖霊（せいれい）からのメッセージです。
あなたが今この本を手にしているということは、
聖霊（せいれい）があなたにこのメッセージを
届（とど）けたいと願（ねが）っているからです。
この本に出会えたことは、
あなたへの聖霊の祝福（しゅくふく）であり奇跡（きせき）です。

この本に書いてあること

- ♥ 子どもの王国（おうこく）とは
- ♥ 旅（たび）のはじまり
  〜たんぽぽの綿毛（わたげ）〜
- ♥ 宝物（たからもの）のこと
- ♥ 幸福（こうふく）になるために
- ♥ 平和（へいわ）のゆくえ🍀

What is reflected in your eyes now?

Do you see your mother, father, and your family?
Do you see your friends and teachers at school?
Do you see the conditions of the Japanese society?
Do you see the unceasing conflicts in this world?
Do you see the destruction of nature on Earth?

Your eyes are the entrance leading to your soul.
I wonder what you see with your eyes, and what is delivered to your soul at this moment.

Your soul is indeed your life, neither your body nor your mind is.
Your soul is larger than your body and mind; it embraces your whole body and mind.
And yet, the soul is invisible, it is difficult to feel, it resides deep in your mind.

The soul is big, yet it is small.

今、あなたの瞳には何がうつりますか？

お父さんやお母さん、家族が見えますか？
学校のお友だちや先生が見えますか？
日本の社会の様子が見えますか？
争いの絶えない世界が見えますか？
壊れていく地球の自然が見えますか？

瞳は、魂に通じる入り口です。
今あなたの瞳に何がうつり、その魂に何が届いているのでしょうね。

魂とは生命そのものであり、
あなたのその体でも その心でもありません。
体と心をすべて包んでいるもっと大きなものです。
でも、それは目に見えず、なかなか感じることもできず、
心の奥に小さく宿っているのです。

大きくもあり、小さいもの です。

When you were a baby, when you were very little, as with children around the world, your soul lived deep within your heart at the same time that it lived in the Kingdom of Children.

In the Kingdom of Children, All is One. Everything is connected. The Kingdom of Children can also be called the Kingdom of God.

A child's soul is protected by God.

A child's soul is innocent. The soul can easily forget anger or sadness; it can easily forgive.

April showers bring May flowers.

In the eyes of little children, people are warm and reliable, everything in the natural world has its soul, and living things in various forms are exciting and wondrous.

The sky, earth, ocean, trees…everything sparkles in their eyes.

A child might even hear the sound of stars in the sky if they live in an area surrounded by beautiful nature.

The inhabitants of the Kingdom of Children are able to see the beauty (mystery) of nature,

and are able to live a life of nowness.

赤ちゃんのころ、小さな子どものころ、
世界中の子どもの魂は、自分の心の奥に住みながら、
同時に子どもの王国に住んでいます。
子どもの王国はすべてが一つ。すべてとつながっています。
それを神の国という人もいます。
子どもたちの魂は、神さまに守られています。

その魂は無垢な魂です。怒りも悲しみもすぐに忘れることができ、人を許すことができる魂です。
小さい子はよく「今泣いたカラスがもう笑った！」と言われますね。
小さな子どもたちの瞳には、人は温かく信じられるものであり、自然界はすべて魂を宿していて、生き物は、さまざまな姿で面白く、不思議です。
空も大地も海も木々もすべてがキラキラして見えます。
暮らしている場所が美しい自然に囲まれていれば、その耳には、空の星の音さえ聞こえる子どももいるでしょう。

子どもの王国の住人は、自然界の美しさ（神秘）を見て、
今という瞬間の時間を生きることができます。

A soul leaves the Kingdom of Children to start a journey, when the hosting body grows up - to around 10 years old, which is just about your age.

You who are at the age of 10 may get frustrated because you feel that your teachers and friends at school are wrong. You may feel anger at your mother and father because what they tell you does not make sense. You may notice that there are too many conflicts among adults in society.

Sometimes, you might get lonely, feeling isolated from the world. You might feel unexplainable anger or sadness. This is because you have become **independent** from the Kingdom of Children. Congratulations! Independence means that you have grown up very healthily. Having grown up healthily, now your **uniqueness has been born.**
Uniqueness means that you are special.

生命(魂)は、それを宿した体が成長すると
子どもの王国を出て、旅に出始めます。
ちょうど10歳くらい。今のあなたですね。

最近、10歳のあなたは、学校で先生やお友達のすることが、
おかしい！と不満をもつことがあるでしょう。
お父さんやお母さんがあなたに言うことに、ちがうよ！と怒りを感じることもあるでしょう。テレビのニュースを見て、社会の中で大人たちが、多くの争いをしていることにも気がつくでしょう。

そして時々、まるで世界でひとりぼっちのようなさみしい気持ちになるかもしれません。よくわからない怒りや悲しみを感じるかもしれません。でもそれは、あなたが子どもの王国から独立をしたからなのです。
おめでとう!! 独立したことは、とてもすこやかな成長です。
すこやかに成長したあなたには、個性が誕生しました。
個性は、オンリー1 という意味です。

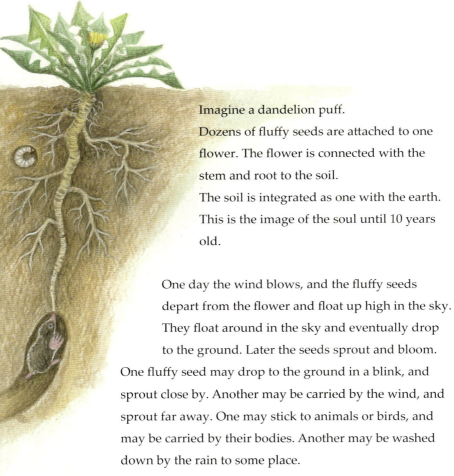

Imagine a dandelion puff.
Dozens of fluffy seeds are attached to one flower. The flower is connected with the stem and root to the soil.
The soil is integrated as one with the earth. This is the image of the soul until 10 years old.

One day the wind blows, and the fluffy seeds depart from the flower and float up high in the sky. They float around in the sky and eventually drop to the ground. Later the seeds sprout and bloom.
One fluffy seed may drop to the ground in a blink, and sprout close by. Another may be carried by the wind, and sprout far away. One may stick to animals or birds, and may be carried by their bodies. Another may be washed down by the rain to some place.
A seed dropped close by does not always sprout soon. A seed which has been carried faraway for a long time might easily bloom, if there is an adequate amount of water and light.
Every fluffy seed is different.

You are now 10 years old, a fluffy dandelion seed floating up high in the sky. You have left the Kingdom of Children, and your soul is about to start a journey through life.

たんぽぽの綿毛を思い描いてください。
綿毛は何十本も一つの花にくっついています。
花は茎と根っこにつながり、土とつながっています。
土は大地で一つにつながっています。
これが10歳までの生命(魂)のイメージです。

綿毛はある時風が吹いて、花から離れて空に舞い上がります。
そして、ふわふわと空を舞って地面に落ちます。
種はその後、芽を出し花を咲かせます。
あっという間に地面に落ち、近くで芽を出す綿毛もあれば、
長く風にのって遠くの大地で芽を出す綿毛もあります。
途中で動物や鳥の体にくっついて移動したり、雨でどこかに流れついていく綿毛もあるでしょう。
すぐ近くに種が落ちてもなかなか芽が出せないこともあります。長い時間遠くまで飛ばされても、ちょうどよい水と光を受けて、すぐ花を咲かせる種もあるでしょう。
それは、様々です。

10歳の今のあなたは、空に舞い上がった一つの綿毛です。
すべてとつながっていた子どもの王国を出て、あなたの生命(魂)は自分の人生の旅に出るのです。

"How was I born?"

"Where does life come from?"

"Who is my mother's mother?"

"Who are my ancestors?"

"When did human beings emerge?"

"How was the world created?"

"Did the earth come into existence 4 billion and 600 million years ago?"

"Was the universe created by the Big Bang?"

You are at the age where you start thinking about such things. History, science, religion…I hope you learn a lot and find your own answers.

Every human being experiences birth and death.

Some people live longer or shorter than others, but death comes to us all. "Where was I before birth, and where will I go after death?" "Why was I born into this world?"
This is a theme for everyone's journey of life.

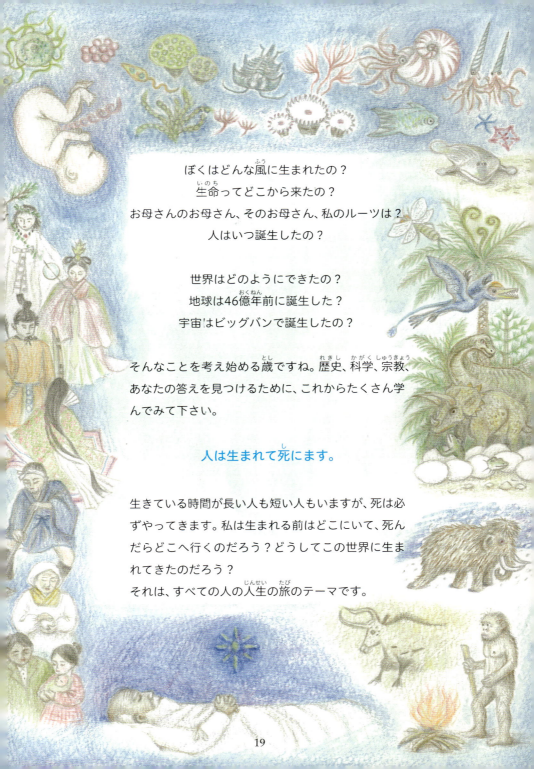

　　　ぼくはどんな風に生まれたの？
　　　生命ってどこから来たの？
　　お母さんのお母さん、そのお母さん、私のルーツは？
　　　　人はいつ誕生したの？

　　　　世界はどのようにできたの？
　　　　地球は46億年前に誕生した？
　　　宇宙はビッグバンで誕生したの？

そんなことを考え始める歳ですね。歴史、科学、宗教、あなたの答えを見つけるために、これからたくさん学んでみて下さい。

　　　　人は生まれて死にます。

生きている時間が長い人も短い人もいますが、死は必ずやってきます。私は生まれる前はどこにいて、死んだらどこへ行くのだろう？どうしてこの世界に生まれてきたのだろう？
それは、すべての人の人生の旅のテーマです。

The journey of life is like a treasure hunt.

"Are there any treasures?" "What is treasure?"
It is veiled in secrecy.
Search for your very own treasures.

All I can tell you is…treasures are brilliant!
Your treasures are not the same as somebody else's.
Treasures are not something you can find in competition.
Some people can find their own treasures during their lives, but others cannot. A person who has found their own treasure might be unaware of it until the end of their life.
Your **soul** can find your life journey's treasures.

It is difficult to feel your soul. However, your soul sends you messages in the forms of **dreams and intuitions**. Please remember…

Keep your eyes clear, keep your ears open, listen carefully to your heart, and you will be able to find your own treasures.

人生の旅は 宝物探しです。

宝物があるの？ 宝物って何でしょう？
それは、秘密のヴェールに包まれています。
あなただけの宝物を探しなさい。

宝物は輝いている！とだけ教えておきましょう。
その宝物は人と同じではありません。だから競って見つけるものでは
ないのです。宝物は、人生で見つけられる人もいれば、見つけられない
人もいます。見つけていたのにそのことに気づかないで人生を終える
人もいます。宝物は人生の旅で、魂によって見つけることができるのです。

魂は自分では感じられにくいものです。でも、夢や直感という形でメッ
セージをくれます。覚えておいてください。

澄んだ瞳で、耳を澄ませ、心を澄ませば
宝物を見つけられます。

There is a purpose in life. What is it?

The answer is **to achieve happiness**.

Every person in the world wishes to be happy, and lives in search for happiness.

Happiness differs from person to person.

Some people would be happy if they are healthy. Some people would be happy if they have a family. Some would be happy with a small amount of money. Some would be happy when they live in harmony with nature. Some would be happy when they are drawing, playing music, or enjoying art.

Some think that happiness is to be rich. Some think that happiness is to do good for others.

People have different ideas of happiness. Besides, a person may actually feel happiness from something else other than their idea of what happiness is. Even so, people do their best to achieve happiness.

人生には目的があります。人生の目的は何でしょう？
それは幸福になることです。
世界中の人が幸せになりたいと願い、幸福を求めて生きています。

幸福は人それぞれ違います。
健康であれば幸福な人もいます。家族がいれば幸福な人もいます。少しのお金があれば幸福な人もいます。
自然と共生していれば幸福な人もいます。絵がかければ、音楽ができれば、芸術にふれていれば幸福な人もいます。
お金持ちになることが幸福だと思っている人もいます。
人の役に立つことが幸福だと思う人もいます。

幸福だと考えることは、人それぞれ違います。そして、幸福だと考えていたことと、実際に幸福だと感じることも時に違います。
でも、人はそのために一生懸命生きていきます。

Whether in a wealthy country or in a poor country, people make a living as a foundation for happiness. What should you do from now on to build a strong foundation?

☆**Study hard whenever you are given a learning environment. Knowledge is a tool you can use in your journey of life. Having many tools will be helpful in many ways.**

☆**Build a strong and healthy body. A strong and healthy body is valuable, because you will be walking alone through your journey. Therefore, know the importance of what you eat.**

☆**Cooperate with others. A single person's ability is limited. However, bigger achievements can be made if people work together. Therefore, build trust with other people.**

As you are ten, I wish for you to do your best in these three areas every day.

豊かな国にいても、貧しい国にいても、人はまず、暮らしを成り立たせることを、幸福の土台とします。その土台を作るためには、あなたはこれから何をすべきでしょう。

☆学べる環境があるなら、たくさん勉学に励みなさい。
　勉学の知識は人生の旅の道具(ツール)となります。道具(ツール)をたくさん持っていると、様々な場面で役に立ちます。

☆丈夫な体を作りなさい。一人で歩く旅は、強い体が何よりです。そのために、口に入れる食物の大切さを知りなさい。

☆人と協力しなさい。一人ではできないことも、人が力を合わせると、大きなことができるようになります。そのために、人との信頼を築きなさい。

10歳のあなたは、この3つのことを毎日の生活の中で努力していきましょう。

These three areas will be your foundation in seeking happiness.

If you make efforts in the three areas every day, you will notice that by doing so you are valuing your mind and body, or yourself. You are valuing what surrounds you just as much as yourself.

To value something means **to care for** something. People "care for" what they value. People often say "I care for my family." or "Take care."

To care for something means to **LOVE** something.

LOVE is not a very familiar word to Japanese people, but in the Western world (especially in Christianity) it is used all the time.

この3つのことを土台に、あなたは幸福を深めることができます。
あなたは、この3つのことを毎日努力していくうちに気がつくでしょう。
それは、「自分自身を大切にしていくということ」
そして、「周りのものも自分と同じように大切にしていくということ」です。

大切にすることは、大事にすることです。大切だと思うものは、「だいじだいじ！」と言いますね。
よくおじいさんが「うちのだいじな子、だいじな孫」と言ったりもしますね。
「おだいじに」という言葉もよく使われます。

大事にすることは、愛することと同じ意味です。
愛という言葉は日本人には、あまりなじみがありませんが、西洋では(とくにキリスト教では)愛という言葉がよく使われます。

Love all

It may be difficult. If so, try to love all. Love is born simply by trying.

When you once lived in the Kingdom of Children, you grew up absorbing love. **LOVE** is the air of the Kingdom of Children. Because you grew up absorbing love, it is not that difficult to love if you try. It is like breathing. You are able to love naturally.

Love the universe, the earth, and the natural world where all beings exist. Try to love people around you.

すべてを愛するようにしましょう。

それはむずかしいことかもしれません。それなら、すべてを愛するように心がけましょう。心がけるだけでも愛は生まれます。

あなたは子どもの王国に住んでいた時、愛を吸って育ちました。子どもの王国の空気は、愛なのです。愛を吸って大きくなったあなたは、心がければ、愛するということは、さほどむずかしいことではありません。
呼吸といっしょです。本来は、自然にできるはずです。

宇宙を地球を、生命宿るものすべての自然界を愛しましょう。
周囲にいる人を愛するよう心がけましょう。

Let's get back to **the story of treasures.**

The chance to find your treasures will come to you several times during your journey of life. You will notice if you pay attention.
You will hear the voice of your soul. You may hear the voice at difficult times of your life, or at times when you are experiencing happiness. The timing differs from person to person. You cannot obtain your treasures unless you go on an adventure. **Courage and action** is necessary for an adventure.

It might seem extremely difficult. Your mother and father might not approve of your idea. You might get left out by others. You might experience pain and suffering.
Even so, you definitely have the **ability** to obtain your treasures, because they are your very own. Have courage, take action, and it will **open the way.**
Believe in your ability, and work hard with all your heart.

宝物のことに、話をもどしましょう。

宝物を見つけるチャンスは、人生を歩んでいる途中で、何度か現れます。注意深くしていると気がつきます。
魂の声がするのです。その声は、もしかすると、苦しくつらい時に聞こえるかもしれないし、とても幸せだと感じて過ごしている時に聞こえるかもしれません。どんな時かは人それぞれです。
そして、宝物というのは、冒険をしなければ手に入りません。
冒険には、勇気と行動がいります。

それは、とても困難に見えるかもしれません。お父さんやお母さんが反対するかもしれません。仲間外れになるかもしれません。痛い思いや苦しい思いをするかもしれません。
でも、あなたは宝物を手に入れる力を必ず持っているのです。
なぜなら、それはあなたの宝物なのですから。
勇気を出して行動したときに、道は開けます。
そして、自分の力を信じて、ひたすら一心に取り組むのです。

In the course of obtaining your treasures, you will go through trials and temptations. There are many people who miss their chances one step away from their treasures. Let me advise you.

Handle money with care.
In our time money has a huge amount of energy. Money is very useful, but you may lose your treasures if you use it in the wrong way. It is not right to consider money at hand more important than your treasures. You will definitely understand this at the end of your life.

Choose your words with care.
From old times people have believed that words have spirits. Words also have energy. Use good words and words filled with love, but not dirty words.
The energy of words connects to all. It connects to the elements composing the universe, which are earth, water, fire, wind, and void; and this **brings luck** to you.
Be connected to all, so that your soul is kept protected.
In the Kingdom of Children you had been connected to all.
Uplift your luck and attract good fortune.

宝物を手に入れるためには、試練や誘惑がやってきます。あと一歩というところで、宝物を逃してしまう人もたくさんいます。アドバイスをしておきましょう。

お金に注意しなさい。

今の時代、お金は人生において大きなエネルギーであり、とても役に立ちますが、使い方を間違えると宝物は失われます。宝物よりも、目の前のお金がいいと思うのは間違いです。それは人生の最後になったときに必ずわかります。

そして、言葉に注意しなさい。

昔から言霊（ことだま）という言葉があるように、言葉には魂が宿ります。言葉もエネルギーです。汚い言葉を使わず、よい言葉や愛のこもった言葉を使うのです。

言葉のエネルギーは、すべてとつながります。この世界を構成している元素の地水火風空のエネルギーとつながり運をもたらすものです。すべてとつながり、魂が守られるようになさい。子どもの王国ではすべてとつながっていました。運気をあげて、幸運を引き寄せるようにするのです。

Do you know why I have told you the story of treasures? It is because you are shining brilliantly at the age of 10. Your body and mind have **strength and courage**, and they are very **pure**. At the beginning of your journey, you will hear the first voice of your soul telling you where your treasure is. At the age of ten, you can find hints in your everyday life. The fact that you are reading this book now is one of these hints given to you.

Let me tell you a famous story of the astronaut who was the first man to land on the moon. When he was a child, he was enjoying a moonlight stroll with his family and said, "I will go to that moon some day!" Back then a rocket flying to the moon was beyond imagination. His father and mother listened to his innocent words with a smile. However, the **soul** of the astronaut knew where his treasure was. It knew that he would find the treasure 30 years later.

Children's **words about dreams** often come true. This means words from boys and girls of your age.

なぜ、宝物の話をあなたにしたのか分かりますか？
10歳のあなたは、美しく輝いているからです。
あなたの体と心は、力も勇気もあり、とても純粋です。
宝物のありかを教える最初の魂の声は、まず、旅の初めに聞こえます。10歳の今のあなたの毎日に、ヒントがあります。
この本を手にしたことも、ヒントの一つです。

有名な話をしましょう。人類で初めて月面着陸を果たした宇宙飛行士は、子どものころ、月の明るい夜に家族で散歩していて、「ぼくはいつかあの月に行く！」と話したそうです。当時、ロケットが月に飛んで行くなどということは、まだ考えられなかった時代です。お父さんもお母さんも子どもの無邪気な言葉を笑って聞いていました。でも、その宇宙飛行士の魂は知っていたのです。その魂の宝物のあるところを。そして、30年後に宝物を見つけることを。

子どもが夢を語る言葉は、よく現実になります。
それは、今のあなたと同じ年頃です。

Today, the age in which you live, a flood of information from the internet has put the society and world into confusion.
You live in an age when it is difficult to hear the **voice of your soul**.
"What do I want to do in my future?" "What is happiness?" You might get more confused as you grow up into an adult. If that happens, I hope you recall what is written in this book.

When you get lost, your mother and father and people around you might give you advice based on their ideas. However, you are the one who is making the journey of your life. You are the one who experiences the feeling of happiness. Rely on the voice of your soul.

When you find your treasures, you will feel so happy like you are in heaven. Treasures are that **powerful**. Therefore, it is **very important** to search for your treasures.

Your soul will find your treasures. If your soul is **freed**, it becomes easier to find your treasures.

今、あなたが生きている時代は、インターネットなどにより情報がたくさんあり、社会も世界も混迷しています。

あなたは、魂の声をきくことがむずかしくなっている時代に生きています。

ぼくは将来何がしたいのだろう？ 幸せって何？ とこれから大人になっていくほどわからなくなったりするでしょう。

そんな時、この本を思い出して下さい。

あなたが迷った時、お父さんやお母さん、周りの人は、自分の考えのアドバイスをしてくれるでしょう。でも、あなたの人生の旅は、あなたが歩むものです。幸福もあなたが感じるのです。

魂の声をたよりになさい。

宝物を見つけると、きっとあなたはとても幸福を感じます。宝物にはそういう力があるのです。だから、人生で幸せになるために、宝物を探すことはとても重要なのです。

宝物は魂が見つけます。魂は自由になると、宝物を見つけやすくなります。

自由に生きなさい。

You might now feel, "this book doesn't make sense…" However, your soul must have understood. Your soul is much wiser than you think. Your soul knows a lot because it has been learning from long before you were born.

Believe in the strength of your soul,

lead a good life,

and you will receive the blessings of God♡

If many children's souls live their lives filled with joy of searching for their own treasures, the world will become a peaceful place. Because your soul is eternal and All is One. It neither battles nor harms.

(a message from the Holy Spirit)

この本に書かれていることは、
今のあなたは、「意味がわからない…」と思うことでしょう。
でも、この本を読んだあなたの魂は、理解したはずです。あなたの魂は、あなたが考えているよりもずっと賢いのです。それは、あなたが生まれるずっと前から多くを学んで知っているからです。

自分の魂の力を信じて、

よい人生を歩みなさい。

きっと神さまから祝福を受けることでしょう♡

多くの子どもたちの魂が、自分の宝物を探すことを楽しみにして人生を歩めば、世界は平和になるはずです。なぜなら、生命（魂）は永遠であり、すべては一つだから。
争ったり傷つけたりはしないのです。

（聖霊からのメッセージ）

あとがき

Prema 陽子

私は、自分の魂の声をきいてこの本を書きました。
私には、今10歳の誕生日を迎える息子がいます。
息子の人生を想い深く願うことは、**幸せな豊かな人生を送ってほしい**ということです。その願いは、世界共通のすべての母の願いでもあるでしょう。
子どもの魂が深いところで子どもの王国につながっているように、母の魂も深いところで母の王国につながっています。この聖霊からのメッセージは、世界中の母たちの願いを叶えていくものになるでしょう。

私はこの本を書くことで、私の人生の宝物を一つ手に入れることができました。宝物は確かに輝いていて、それを手にした時、魂がわくわく歓びに満ちます♡
そして、このような本を書いて、人に読んでもらうということを決心するときに、勇気もいりました。
私自身も私の人生の旅を歩み、宝物探しをしている最中です。

誰の人生も人生の主役は自分です。私は母として、わが子の魂の力を信じて見守ることができればと思います。

Prema 陽子は3人います。

文を書いた陽子。英訳をした陽子。絵を描いた陽子。

3人は「マザーハウス」という2000年〜2008年に愛知県みよし市に存在した私設の小さな保育施設で出会いました。たくさんの人がボランティアで支え、愛のもとに存在していた、子どものための施設です。

Prema（プレマ）というのはサンスクリット語の愛という意味です。

この本は、3人の母の愛が結晶した本です。

最後になりますが、私はこのメッセージを書くのに、聖霊、祝福、奇跡、神、言霊、愛、魂、などの言葉を用いました。私の言葉の表現や使い方に、気分を害される方もいらっしゃるかもしれません。どうぞ、寛容な心でお許し下さい。私自身は、特定の宗教を信仰していませんが、魂の声をきいてインスピレーションを受けてこの本を書きました。このメッセージの内容は、多くの宗教に共通するものでもあるでしょう。

国境、宗教の壁を越えて、多くの人の心に届くことを願っています。

どうぞ皆様の心の中の純粋な『10歳の心』に届きますように・・・

2019年 春

Afterword

Yoko Prema

I have listened to the voice of my soul and wrote this book.

I have a son who is about to have his 10th birthday.

When I think of my son's life, **I deeply wish for him to lead a happy and enriched life**. This wish is universal, a wish common to all parents in this world.

As a child's soul is deeply connected to the Kingdom of Children, a mother's soul is deeply connected to the Kingdom of Mothers. This message from the Holy Spirit will fulfill the wishes of mothers across the world.

I have obtained one treasure of my life by writing this book.

This treasure was definitely shining brilliantly, and I was filled with joy when I found it♡ It took courage to decide to write this kind of book for people to read. I am also in the course of my journey of life, searching for my own treasures.

Everybody plays the leading role of their life. As a mother, I hope I am able to believe the strength of my child's soul, and watch him grow and learn.

There are three Yoko Premas.

Yoko who wrote the text. Yoko who translated it into English.

Yoko who drew the illustration. The three of us met at a small private childcare facility called "Mother House", which existed from 2000 to 2008 in Miyoshi City, Aichi Prefecture. This childcare facility was supported by many volunteers, and it was a place full of love. Prema means love in Sanskrit. This book is an embodiment of love of the three mothers.

Finally, I am most grateful for your generosity in accepting my wording in this message, such as the Holy Spirit, blessing, miracle, God, spirits of words, love, and soul. My expressions and wording may offend some people's feelings. I do not practice a specific religion, but I wrote this book because I heard the voice of my soul and got inspirations. The content of this message is common to many religions.

I sincerely hope that this message transcends the national borders and religious differences, and reaches the hearts of many people. May this message reach your pure 10-year-old heart…

Spring, 2019

If this book is passed to you by somebody, please color in one♡. (One good thing may happen to you☆) If you are the first person, please also sign your name in the angel's flag.

When you are finished, please pass the book on to somebody else, so that one book is read by 100 people.

あなたのもとに、この本がめぐって来たら
♡に1つあなたの色を塗ってください。
（きっと1つ良いことがおきるでしょう★彡）
1番目の人は天使のはたにサインも書いてくださいね✏
そして、あなたが読み終えたら、
この本をどなたかに渡して旅をさせてあげてください。
たんぽぽの綿毛のように…！

さんからスタート

1冊の本が100人にめぐりますように♥
お家の方へ🏠この本は書店又はAmazonでお求めいただくことができます

10歳のあなたと10歳だったあなたへ
～聖霊からのおくりもの～

Dear 10-year-olds And Former 10-year-olds
~a gift from the Holy Spirit~

2019年9月3日 初版発行

著　者　Prema 陽子
　　　　（文／浅沼陽子　英訳／永合陽子　絵／甲斐田陽子）
定　価　本体価格1,600円＋税
発行所　株式会社　三恵社
　　　　〒462-0056 愛知県名古屋市北区中丸町2-24-1
　　　　TEL 052-915-5211　FAX 052-915-5019
　　　　URL http://www.sankeisha.com

本書を無断で複写・複製することを禁じます。乱丁・落丁の場合はお取替えいたします。
Ⓒ2019 Prema Yoko　ISBN 978-4-86693-119-7 C0012 ¥1600E